WELCOME

TO WORSHIP IN THE WILDERNESS

"Whoever claims to live in him must live as Jesus did." (1 John 2:6).

Part of living as Jesus did must involve us following him into the wilderness. He invites us to journey with him through forty days of testing, prayer, reflection and transformation. This series of seven services, and the accompanying *Personal Devotions* book, are designed to help you and your congregation walk though this Spirit-filled, sacrificial and surprising journey together.

Wilderness in the Bible

In scripture, wilderness does not have one simple meaning. Instead, it is a rich metaphor which holds various things in tension. On the most basic level the desert was a dry, lifeless and lawless place, which made the Israelites confront their fears, frailty and mortality. Their experience after the Exodus, when they persistently disobeyed God and were punished, also added a layer of guilt and repentance to their mental picture of the wilderness.

In the face of these "negative" associations with the desert, the Israelites also saw it as a place of provision, transformation and encounter with God. Countless characters including Jacob, Hagar, Job, David and Elijah met with God in the wilderness. This leads Jenny Phillips to write:

"The wilderness of the Bible is a liminal space—an in-between place where ordinary life is suspended, identity shifts, and new possibilities emerge. Through the experiences of the Israelites in exile, we learn that while the biblical wilderness is a place of danger, temptation and chaos, it is also a place for solitude, nourishment, and revelation from God."

Jenny Phillips, "Jesus and Wilderness"
http://bibleresources.americanbible.org/resource/jesus-and-wilderness

Wilderness in our lives

In today's church we may not be very confident in addressing themes such as sorrow, guilt or doubt. Yet these kinds of thoughts and experiences surround our congregations every day. It might be that our jobs, homes or communities feel like a place of barren exile. We can experience the wilderness of losing a loved one, being fired or getting ill. Or it might be that our inner worlds are the desert places, as we go through periods of feeling dry, doubtful or depressed. Michael Card writes:

"The wilderness is still the place of worship. But for you and me it is not a matter of dunes and dry ground; in fact, it may be deceptively green. Our hunger and thirst are more spiritual realities than physical ones. The desolation we often experience involves our yearning for a more palpable feeling of the Presence of God. We need spiritual bread every bit as much as they needed the manna in the wilderness. Our deep need for Living Water is just as intense as any thirst their parched throats ever knew."

Michael Card,
A Sacred Sorrow, page 24.

Perhaps some people in our congregations are yet to experience these things. It may be that in helping them journey with Jesus you can prepare them for future struggles.

Wilderness worship

One discovery we will make is that wilderness worship might look different to "mountaintop" worship. It can involve biblical practices such as fasting and giving. We can learn from the Desert Mothers and Fathers of the 4th Century, in their experiences of silence, simplicity and solitude. It can encompass emotions which we do not normally sing or pray about - grief, doubt, complaint. This may involve you learning some new songs, new ways of praying or more ancient forms of spirituality. As Pete Greig puts it:

> "Where, I wonder, is the mystery and the mess of biblical spirituality? What place is there in our happy-clappy culture for the disturbing message of books such as Ecclesiastes, Lamentations and Job? Where are the moments in both our private and public meetings with God when the major key turns to the minor, when the soft rock anthems pay respect to the blues, and when those top melodies of pop praise finally give way to the scattered logic of jazz?"

Pete Greig, *God on Mute*, pages 101-102.

Using this book

To help you with all this, we have prepared seven service outlines. Each centres around two key Bible passages (usually one Old Testament and one Gospel reading), and a unifying theme. There are also numerous ideas for prayer, creativity, songs, hymns and responses. You will need to adapt each of these to suit your context. It may also be important to include other worship elements from your own tradition.

Some more specific pointers:

Downloadable material: Small icons on each page show where PowerPoints, videos, PDF and Word documents can be downloaded. Visit **www.engageworship.org/wilderness** and use the password **XF4PP32B**. Feel free to share this password with other people in your own church, but please do not share it beyond your congregation. Other churches need to purchase this book to qualify for the free downloads. Also be aware that some of the downloadable resources may be sold on other pages of our website, so only use www. engageworship.org/wilderness to ensure you are not paying for your free material.

Sermon outlines: These have been written to be adapted for your context. You can download editable Word documents to be able to add stories, additional Bible content or rearrange further. There is also a downloadable PowerPoint for each sermon. Note the blank slide at the end of the presentation - this is for you to be able to add your own headings, quotes etc.

Songs and hymns: We have suggested music for each week. Visit **www.engageworship.org/ wilderness** for a full list with links to videos and sheet music wherever possible. For most churches it is difficult to add too many new songs over a short period, so consider carefully what is already in your repertoire. It may be best to decide on a few "theme songs" which you will use most weeks - for example Sam's "You Lead Us Through The Wilderness" which is printed on the last page of this book.

Using the Personal Devotions

We have also published a book of personal devotions to accompany this series. You could buy this book in bulk to sell or give away to your congregation. *Worship in the Wilderness: Personal Devotions* has five reflections for each week up to Palm Sunday, with various prayerful, creative and practical responses. The material could also be adapted as small group discussions and activities. Visit **www.engageworship. org/wilderness** to get hold of the book.

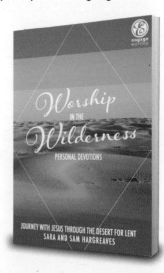

Ash Wednesday

A SECRET JOURNEY

"Don't tear your clothing in your grief, but tear your hearts instead."
(Joel 2:13, NLT)

GATHERING IDEAS

Spoken prayer:

God who made us from the dust and ashes,
breathe into us your breath of life.
God who is kind and compassionate,
welcome us with your forgiveness.
God who knows our frailty first-hand,
lead us through the wilderness
of transformation,
for your glory, Amen.

Visual introduction:

A looping PowerPoint or video with images and Bible texts to introduce the ideas and spirituality of Ash Wednesday. You could pair this with recorded or live music, or silence. Images below are two example slides.

'Create in me a pure heart, O God, and renew a steadfast spirit within me.'
(Ps 51:3)

'So when you give to the needy, do not announce it with trumpets.'
(Matt 6:2)

Psalm 103 worship flow:

This block of worship follows the flow of the psalm, including sung elements, praise, a confession prayer, receiving forgiveness and intercession. In keeping with Ash Wednesday the psalm reminds us that "we are dust". You will need to prepare someone to read verses 6-12, and decide on appropriate music for your setting. You can also decide whether your context is right to create space for open prayers, or whether it would be better to invite people to pray in their hearts, or in small groups.

SLIDE 1 [*Leader says Ps. 103:1*]

SLIDE 2 [*Sing "Praise the Lord" (chorus of "To God be the Glory", Fanny Crosby) or alternative.*]

SLIDE 3 [*Say together Ps. 103:2-5*]

[*Leader says:*]
Here the Psalmist is encouraging himself to remember all the things that God has done for him. These things will inspire his soul to praise God wholeheartedly. So let's take a moment to remember what God has done for us.

SLIDES 4-8 [*Click PowerPoint to highlight each bullet*]:
• Bring to mind the ways God has forgiven you.
• In what ways has God healed you, or someone you know?
• Has there been some sort of "pit of despair", an area of your life you had lost hope in and yet God has turned it around?
• How have you known God's love and compassion recently?
• What good things has God blessed you with?

[*Leader introduces prayer:*]
With those thoughts in mind, feel free to offer up open prayers of thanks to God.

SLIDE 9 [*Sing "Praise the Lord" (chorus of "To God be the Glory") or alternative.*]

SLIDE 10 [*A different reader reads Ps. 103:6-12*]

[*Leader says:*]

Let's take some time in silence to remember any sins which we may need to confess before God today, trusting in his promise that he does not repay us what we deserve, but that he is gracious and compassionate, removing our sins as far as the East is from the West.

[*Silence for confession*]

SLIDE 11 [*Sing "The Lord is Gracious and Compassionate" by Graham Ord, or alternative forgiveness song.*]

SLIDE 12 [*Leader says:*]
Let's read the next verses silently, and allow God to remind us of friends and family, or situations that we are aware of, which need God's compassion. As things come to mind I would encourage you to pray for those situations, praying for God's love to shine through in hard places.

[*Read Ps. 103:13-19 silently*]

[*Silence for prayer*]

SLIDE 13 [*Leader says:*]
Let's declare these final words of the Psalm together, as praise to God:

[*Read Ps. 103:20-22*]

> Praise the Lord, my soul,
>   and forget not all his benefits—
> who forgives all your sins
>   and heals all your diseases,
> who redeems your life from the pit
>   and crowns you with love and compassion,
> who satisfies your desires with good things
>   so that your youth is renewed like the eagle's.
>
> Psalm 103:2-5

Poem/prayer:

Written by Richard Lyall, used with permission.

In what we have done
and neglected to do,
in the good we intended
but not followed through:
[*All*]: **Lord, we have fallen.**

[*Pause in silence*]

For our wandering off
and forgetting your ways;
for leaving you out
of our moments, our days:
[*All*]: **Lord, we are sorrowful.**

[*Pause in silence*]

[*All*]: **Lord, in dust and in ashes
we turn our hearts back to you
and seek your forgiveness.
Lord, have mercy,
Christ, have mercy,
Lord have mercy.**

[*Pause in silence*]

From the ashes you lift us,
erasing our shame.
You grant fresh beginnings
and restore us again.
[*All*]: **Lord, you have raised us.**

[*Pause in silence*]

Lord you draw us back to you
and forgive us our wrongs.
You replace our lamenting
with worshipful songs.
[*All*]: **Lord, we are grateful.**

[*Pause in silence*]

HEARING GOD'S WORD

Bible readings:

Joel 2:1-2, 12-16.

Matthew 6:1-6, 16-18.

Sermon outline:

Today marks the beginning of Lent. We will be following Jesus into the desert, engaging in a series called Worship in the Wilderness. We'll be exploring the idea that wilderness worship can look quite different to other forms of worship we might be familiar with - it can involve things like fasting, solitude, simplicity and sacrifice.

These forms of worship are given to us by God in the Bible. In both New and Old Testaments the people of God were called to come to him in times of repentance, simplicity and sorrow. But God has some words of caution before we embark on this wilderness journey.

1) A time to rend our hearts

The prophet Joel warns the people of God's coming judgement. He calls them to a period of repentance, of fasting, weeping and mourning. Part of our Lent journey will involve us acknowledging the broken world that we live in, and the mistakes that we all make which contribute to that brokenness. Like the people in Joel's time, we may need to turn to God to confess the sin in the world and the sin in our own lives. We may find it appropriate to fast, weep or mourn. As we do so, we will find that God continues to be gracious, compassionate, slow to anger and abounding in love.

In the midst of this message Joel has an important warning. He says "rend your hearts, not your garments". Or in the New Living Translation:

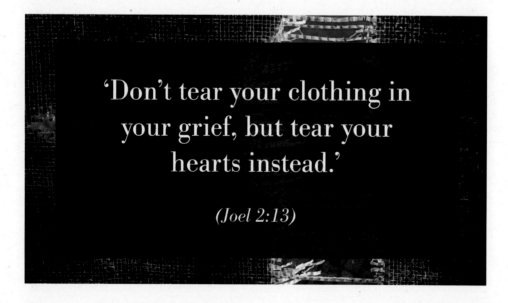

'Don't tear your clothing in your grief, but tear your hearts instead.'

(Joel 2:13)

As with any act of worship, it is always possible to put on an "outward show" of engagement with God, while our hearts are somewhere else. We can sing the right songs, pretend to be spiritual, or talk loudly about how much fasting we're doing. But all this means very little if it is motivated by selfish desires, rather than a broken and contrite heart before God.

2) A time in the secret place

Jesus takes this warning a stage further. He challenges his hearers not to engage in spiritual practices "to be seen by others" or "to be honoured by others". He too is concerned that practices like giving to the needy, prayer and fasting can become ways of showing off. So he encourages us instead to do these things "in secret". He repeats three times that if we do these things in secret:

'Your Father, who sees what is done in secret, will reward you.'

(Matt 6:18)

Now, to be practical for a moment, it is unlikely that any of us can really grow in these spiritual disciplines if we keep them completely secret. Husbands and wives will probably need to talk about things like giving money out of the family budget. If a child wants to fast a meal they will probably need to tell their parents. And even times of prayer will probably involve letting people in your house know you are not to be disturbed.

Beyond this, it can be encouraging to discuss with close friends, a small group or other Christian believers our experiences of these kinds of Lent disciplines. I don't think Jesus' point was that we keep elaborate secrets from each other. His point is to check our hearts, our motives. We need to come into this season asking God to work in us from the inside-out.

3) A time to take something up

If you ask the average person on the street what Lent is about, they will probably talk about giving up chocolate, or alcohol, or some other unhealthy food or habit. And if you know anyone who has done that for Lent, you will probably remember them talking endlessly about how difficult it was and how they suffered for the forty days (or gave up after a week)!

Jesus and Joel set us a different kind of challenge for Lent. Rather than loudly giving things up for Lent, how about we quietly take something up for Lent? Why don't we take the hand of Jesus and be led by the Spirit into the wilderness, as he teaches us the way of simplicity, sorrow, sacrifice and truth-speaking. Let's make this a journey which starts in our hearts, in our deepest desires to follow Jesus, to learn from him and be surprised by where he takes us.

MUSIC IDEAS

Hymns:

- *Sunday's Palms are Wednesday's Ashes* - Rae E. Whitney
- *Forgive us When our Deeds Ignore* - Martin Leckebusch
- *From the Deep Places, Hear my Cry* - Timothy Dudley-Smith

Songs:

- *Ashes* - Mia Fildes, Jason Ingram
- *Simplicity* - Rend Collective
- *You Lead us Through The Wilderness* - Sam Hargreaves
- *Most Merciful God* - Chris Pearce
- *The Lord is Gracious and Compassionate* - Graham Ord

RESPONSE IDEAS

Ashes of lament:

Written by Kieran Metcalfe, used with permission.

Before the service, cover a table with clean, white paper (a roll of lining paper works well). Place a glass bowl on the table filled with ashes from a cooled barbecue or other source.

While using the corporate prayer of confession and lament below, have someone carefully pour out the ashes to cover as much of the white paper as possible.

[*Leader:*]
Father God, your knowledge of us is perfect - the situations we face, the decisions we make, our motives, our passions, our desires.

We long to act justly, but so often sin stains our deeds, just as dust and ashes smear and discolour that which was clean.

So we pour out these ashes, watching them cover the bright clean surface beneath, and we remember the ways in which we have failed to live by your standards.

[*All:*]
Your plan, obscured by our selfish motives.
Your light, smothered by things we wish to hide.
Your love, made fruitless by our inaction.
Your world, tainted by our sin.

[*Leader:*]
We acknowledge, and cry out in shame for our part in the wider issues that affect our world. With these ashes of lament, we remember:

[*All:*]
The world's poor, kept poor by our wasteful lifestyles.
Creation's beauty, marred by our selfish carelessness.
The innocent, caught in the middle of unjust conflicts.

[*Leader:*]
In all these things, our personal, national and global failings, we call out to you to act, to renew, to forgive. To restore the brightness of your love, and the radiance of your glory. We receive your forgiveness that pours from the cross. We receive your empowering to act justly, love mercy, and walk humbly with you.

[*All:*] **Amen.**

During the next part of the service (where you might sing, or play some instrumental music) invite people to come forward and draw a cross, a heart, or any symbol that is appropriate to them in the ashes. This lets the lightness of the paper shine through the darkness of the ashes, as a symbol of asking God to bring his light and hope into the situations you have been reflecting on.

Cross symbol in ashes:

It is traditional to mix ashes (made from burning last year's palm crosses) with a small drop of oil, and to invite the congregation to take the mark of the cross on their forehead. This is a powerful symbol of entering into the season of Lent - embracing repentance, lament, and walking the wilderness-way of the cross with Jesus for forty days.

You may wish to engage with this in your service. Another idea might follow up on the "secret" theme of the sermon - you could invite people to pick up a small piece of paper or card (credit-card sized), and receive the mark of the cross on this paper. They could then put it in a pocket, a phone case or a wallet, as a "secret" reminder of following Jesus through the wilderness.

SENDING IDEA

Sending prayer:

Father God,
you see our secret acts of worship,
you know our hidden sacrifices,
you reward our quiet obedience.
Send us out to live for you,
in the power of your Spirit
and in the name of your Son, Jesus Christ,
Amen.

First Sunday

A SPIRIT-LED JOURNEY

"Let my people go that they may worship me in the wilderness"
(Exodus 7:16)

GATHERING IDEAS

Spoken prayer:

God of feasting and fasting,
mountaintop and desert,
you gather us together by your Holy Spirit.
May we follow Jesus into the wilderness,
feeding on your living bread
and tasting your water of life.
We come hungry and thirsty
for more of you, God. Amen.

"Blessed Be" introduction:

This PowerPoint features images based on lyrics from Matt and Beth Redman's song. Invite the congregation to think about the different kinds of roads they have walked down to get to the service today. You could invite people to share this with the person next to them.

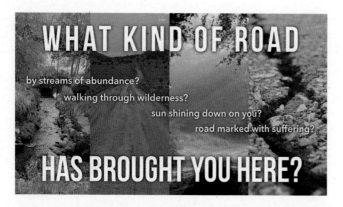

Then pray the gathering prayer together, which could lead into singing "Blessed Be Your Name".

[Leader:] We say together:
[All:] **If you're splashing in streams of abundance,
  we welcome you – share your joy.
If you're parched in a desert wasteland,
  we welcome you – share your doubts.
If you're relaxing in the light of contentment,
  we welcome you – share your peace.
If you're stumbling on a road of suffering,
  we welcome you – share your pain.**
[Leader:] We pray together:
[All:] **God of water, earth, light and brokenness
  we welcome you, as you welcome us.
Amen.**

ALL-AGE IDEA

"Wilderness Grumbling":

Written by Bob Hartman, used with permission.

This reading engages all ages with the story of the Manna in the wilderness. Break your crowd into three groups, one for the people of Israel, one for God, and one for Moses and Aaron. Teach each group their rhyming lines.

[People of Israel:]
**Meatpots in the morning,
white bread, wheat and rye.
We ate our fill in Egypt,
but now we're going to die!**

[God:]
**"Heaven's bread" at daybreak,
"Quail Surprise" at dusk.
I'll send enough for just one day
to teach my people trust.**

[Moses & Aaron:]
**We've had it with your moaning.
We find it rather odd
that you complain to us
instead of grumbling to God.**

You might want to project the words on a screen to help each group remember what to say. Then lead them in those lines at the appropriate time.

Forty-five days after their escape from Egypt, the people of Israel were hungry. So they went to Moses and Aaron and complained.

[People of Israel:] **Meatpots in the morning...**

So Moses went to God and told God what the people had said (as if God didn't know already!). And this is how God replied.

[God:] **"Heaven's bread" at daybreak...**

There was an exception, of course. On the sixth day, the people had to collect two days worth of the food God sent, so they didn't have to do it on the Sabbath.

↓ Downloadable PowerPoint ↓ Downloadable Video W↓ Downloadable Word Doc P↓ Downloadable PDF Script

So Moses and Aaron went back to the people, who were still complaining:

[*People of Israel:*] **Meatpots in the morning...**

In response to which, Moses and Aaron had a moan of their own!

[*Moses & Aaron:*] **We've had it with your moaning...**

And just as Aaron said it, the glory of God appeared in a cloud above the wilderness. And God spoke to Moses and said, "I have heard my people's grumbling, so this is what I shall do:

[*God:*] **"Heaven's bread" at daybreak...**

And, sure enough, quail arrived and covered the camp, that evening. And, sure enough, when the people of Israel woke the next day, they found flaky stuff all over the ground, fine as frost. And even though they did not know exactly what it was, they ate it, and they were no longer hungry.

And, as a result, the moaning of the people...

[*People of Israel:*] **Meatpots in the morning...**

and the frustration of Aaron and Moses...

[*Moses & Aaron:*] **We've had it with your moaning...**

was transformed by God's power and mercy into something they would never forget:

[*God:*] **"Heaven's bread" at daybreak...**

HEARING GOD'S WORD

Bible readings:

Deuteronomy 8:1-5, 15-18. Reflective, visual PowerPoint version of this passage is available (see example slides to the right).

Mark 1:9-13.

Be careful to follow every command I am giving you today, so that you may live and increase and may enter and possess the land the LORD promised on oath to your ancestors.

Deut 8:1

Your clothes did not wear out and your feet did not swell during these forty years. Know then in your heart that as a man disciplines his son, so the LORD your God disciplines you.

Deut 8:4-5

He led you through the vast and dreadful wilderness, that thirsty and waterless land, with its venomous snakes and scorpions. He brought you water out of hard rock.

Deut 8:15

But remember the LORD your God, for it is he who gives you the ability to produce wealth, and so confirms his covenant, which he swore to your ancestors, as it is today.

Deut 8:18

For all free downloads plus song and hymn links, visit www.engageworship.org/wilderness and enter password from page 4.

13

Sermon outline:

Would you agree with me that life has both mountaintop moments and desert days? There are times when you feel on top of the world, and others when it feels like you're just stumbling through the dust. There are times when you feel well fed, comfortable and surrounded by loved ones, and others where you're hungry, thirsty, lonely and tired. In our relationship with God, we have moments when we feel very close to him - perhaps at a Christian conference, a worship event, on a retreat or a holiday. And then we have other days when God seems far away, when we doubt him or struggle with temptations.

If you feel like that, you are not alone. Everyone has these ups and downs, these mountaintop moments and desert days. Not just us today - but even our heroes from the Bible, and even Jesus, experienced both. Our Lent series is going to help us journey with Jesus through the desert wilderness. Today I want to highlight three things that the Bible can teach us about our wilderness experiences.

1) Wilderness is not a sign of God's absence

The people of Israel experienced a huge mountaintop moment. They were led out of slavery in Egypt and then God parted the Red Sea, allowing them to pass and simultaneously destroying their enemies (Ex. 14). They celebrated this by singing a joyful worship song, dancing and playing percussion instruments (Ex. 15). They were on top of the world.

But very quickly in Exodus 15:22-24 they reach a desert or wilderness called Shur, where there is no fresh water. Here their joy turns to grumbling, their worship turns to distrust. They immediately doubt that God is with them. Similarly in chapter 16 they reach another desert called Sin, and here there is no food to eat. They start to long for their days in Egypt, and complain that they are going to die.

Yet in both the deserts of Shur and Sin, God provides for them: with fresh water and with Manna bread and quail meat. Our passage from Deuteronomy shows us the reason why all this happened:

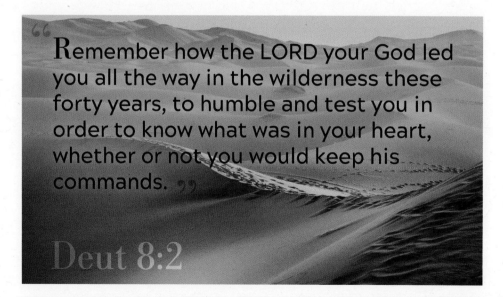

"Remember how the LORD your God led you all the way in the wilderness these forty years, to humble and test you in order to know what was in your heart, whether or not you would keep his commands."

Deut 8:2

When we experience the struggles of the wilderness we should not see them as punishments from God, or signs that God is uncaring or non-existent. Instead we should see that the wilderness is an opportunity for God to test our hearts. Do we really trust in him, or do we trust in our own abilities? As Deuteronomy goes on to say:

> "He gave you manna to eat in the wilderness, something your ancestors had never known, to humble and test you so that in the end it might go well with you. You may say to yourself, 'My power and the

strength of my hands have produced this wealth for me.' But remember the Lord your God, for it is he who gives you the ability to produce wealth, and so confirms his covenant, which he swore to your ancestors, as it is today." (Deuteronomy 8:16-18)

2) We are led by the Spirit into the wilderness

Jesus begins his ministry with a very similar pattern to the people of Israel. He passes through the waters - not the Red Sea, but the waters of baptism in the Jordan river. Again, this is a mountaintop experience, where the Spirit descends and the voice of his Father speaks words of affirmation and devotion: "You are my Son, whom I love; with you I am well pleased." (Mk. 1:11).

We might expect that after this high-point Jesus would launch into his ministry of preaching and demonstrating the Kingdom of God. Yet this is not what happens. Like Israel before him Jesus goes from the waters to the wilderness, from spiritual feasting to the struggle of fasting, from affirmation to loneliness and temptation.

"At once the Spirit sent him out into the wilderness." (Mark 1:12)

Have you experienced that? Moments where you thought God was calling you, sending you, empowering you, followed by setbacks or disappointments? Times of refreshing followed by periods of dryness? If so, take heart that you are following in the footsteps of Jesus. Wilderness is often a place that the Spirit of God leads us to. The Father led Jesus into the desert by the Spirit, and he leads us there too.

3) Wilderness is a place of worship and transformation

Ultimately, God leads us into the wilderness so that we might learn to worship. He says to Pharaoh through Moses:

"Let my people go that they may worship me in the wilderness." (Exodus 7:16)

Worship in the wilderness might look quite different to worship on the mountaintop. It is great to have joyful hymns and songs, to celebrate with banners and colours and hundreds of people. But wilderness worship is often about taking away rather than adding more. It might involve aspects of worship such as fasting, or solitude, or simplicity. It might turn us towards silence, or lament, or giving things away.

All of this might feel a little negative - but imagine this for a moment. [*You could invite people to close their eyes and reflect on this.*] You are walking towards Jesus, and Jesus is reaching out his arms to embrace you. But as you look down your arms are full of stuff. What is it that your arms are full of - the things that you rely on for your worship and your life? Are they full of musical instruments; full of computers or books; full of food and drinks; full of work and activity; full of relationships and family? None of these are bad things, in fact they are gifts of God. But God knows that for us to grow in him we might need to start putting down some of these things we're carrying. Lent and wilderness is about laying down some of these things until we have empty hands. Hands held out ready to receive from him, to be embraced by him.

Some of us may feel we have had wilderness thrust upon us. You might be going through a desert time right now. God is with you, he never wants to see you suffer but he is passionate to see you trust in him, and learn to worship in the wilderness. Others of us may feel great, we might be on mountaintops right now, but even so we can actively choose to learn to worship in wilderness ways. Learning to find God in simplicity will prepare us for whatever lies ahead. Israel was transformed through her wilderness worship. We can be too.

RESPONSE IDEA

Responsive prayer:

[*Leader:*] Sometimes we feel like we're walking through wilderness:
[*All:*] **Jesus we choose to walk with you.**

When our spirits feel dry, help us trust in your Spirit:
Jesus we choose to walk with you.

Fasting seems difficult, prayers seem unanswered:
Jesus we choose to walk with you.

The world howls like wild animals all around us:
Jesus we choose to walk with you.

We can choose to worry, or to trust you to provide:
Jesus we choose to walk with you.

Temptation is everywhere, doubts can overwhelm us:
Jesus we choose to walk with you.

You know what it's like to walk through this desert:
Jesus we choose to walk with you.

You long to transform us with wilderness worship:
Jesus we choose to walk with you. Amen.

SENDING IDEA

Sending prayer:

Holy Spirit,
fill us with your water of life,
so that even as we walk through the desert
we might know your refreshing
and share it with those around us.
Lead us, as you led Jesus,
to the glory of God the Father.
Amen.

MUSIC IDEAS

Songs:

- *You Lead us Through The Wilderness* - Sam Hargreaves
- *Desert Song* - Brooke Ligertwood
- *Out of the Depths* - Rachel Wilhelm
- *Hungry* - Kathryn Scott
- *Blessed Be Your Name* - Matt and Beth Redman
- *40 Days* - Matt Maher

Hymns:

- *Jesus in the Desert* - David Mowbray
- *All the Brown and Bare Horizons* - Christopher Idle
- *The God Who Spoke in Haran* - Christopher Idle
- *Great God, Who Opened up the Sea* - Michael Forster

Second Sunday

A SIMPLE JOURNEY

"... the rich simplicity of
being yourself before God."
(1 Timothy 6:6, MSG)

GATHERING IDEAS

Spoken prayer:

We come to you, faithful Father,
slowing down, taking a deeper breath.
Thank you that we do not need to earn our way into your presence,
but that we can come simply, through Jesus,
by your Holy Spirit.
We pause.
We acknowledge your presence.
We trust you to feed us by your Word. Amen.

Simplified service:

Can you intentionally "simplify" your worship this week? This might involve removing things which are good, but that you can have a habit of depending upon. Exactly *how* you simplify will depend on your normal pattern, but things you could do include:

• Minimal or no use of a projection screen.

• Singing short songs from memory, or scripture songs straight from the Bible

• No instruments, just *a cappella* singing for this week (this may require a strong vocal lead).

• Or, if you usually have a large music group you could simplify down to guitar or piano.

• Speaking out less notices, long prayers or instructions, creating more space for reflection and silence.

• Removing clutter and decorations from the worship space.

ALL-AGE IDEA

Camp worship:

Set up a tent and a fake camp fire in the church. Invite everyone to gather around the fire, and to worship as if you were out in the wilderness with no electricity, screen, hymn books or organs. That might involve one guitar or ukulele, and people suggesting songs that they remember.

Alternatively, you could have this set up outside, and lead people out of the building for a portion of the service.

Silence:

Lead three moments of silence during the service. Explain that the only aim is to rest in God's presence. If it helps, people might like to mouth the name "Jesus" silently. Grow the times of silence, starting with 30 seconds near the beginning of the service. Engage with 1 minute of silence before the talk (possibly after a Bible reading) and 2 minutes after the talk.

In an all-age setting, you might challenge everyone to be as quiet as they can for 30 seconds, then get them to feedback on how it felt, what noises they heard, if they had a sense of God speaking to them or God's presence as they sat in the silence.

HEARING GOD'S WORD

Bible readings:

Psalm 63:1-8. Reflective video version of this passage is available (see examples on this page)

Luke 4:1-13.

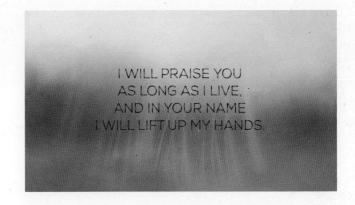

I WILL PRAISE YOU
AS LONG AS I LIVE,
AND IN YOUR NAME
I WILL LIFT UP MY HANDS.

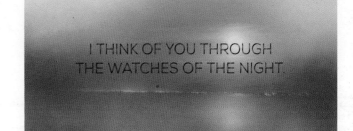

I THINK OF YOU THROUGH
THE WATCHES OF THE NIGHT.

BECAUSE YOU ARE MY HELP,
I SING IN THE SHADOW
OF YOUR WINGS.

Sermon outline:

Last week we introduced the idea of journeying through the wilderness with Jesus for Lent. We talked about how wilderness worship might look different to other kinds of worship we have experienced. Some worship involves singing songs or hymns, using guitars or choirs or organs. Some worship includes prayers that have many words. Some worship requires a lot of technology, or props, or people to make it happen. But wilderness worship is quite different to all of that.

This week we are going to look at three aspects of wilderness worship that Jesus engaged in.

1) Solitude

The first thing we notice about Jesus is that he walked away from the crowds and often spent time alone. In the passage we have read he spends 40 days and nights in this lonely place. Luke also tells of another time when,

> "... the news about him spread all the more, so that crowds of people came to hear him and to be healed of their illnesses. But Jesus often withdrew to lonely places and prayed." (Luke 5:15-16)

We might have different responses to the idea of solitude. Some of us will be very scared of spending time alone - we know that we are extroverts who enjoy people's company and feed off the affirmation of our friends, families and co-workers. Others of us will think that this sounds like a great idea - finally, a bit of privacy; a bit of peace!

Henri Nouwen wrote a book about the Desert Fathers and Mothers - a group of Christians from the 4th and 5th Century who revived the idea of desert spirituality at a time when the church was becoming increasingly institutionalised. Nouwen warns us against seeing solitude as simply as a quiet place to recharge our batteries, and then go on with life as usual. He writes:

> "Solitude is not a private therapeutic place. Rather, it is the place of conversion, a place where the old self dies and the new self is born... In solitude I get rid of my scaffolding: no friends to talk with, no telephone calls to make, no meetings to attend, no music to entertain, no books to distract... We enter into solitude first of all to meet our Lord and to be with him and him alone."
>
> Henri Nouwen,
> *The Way of The Heart*, p. 27, 30.

The main reason Jesus sought solitude was to be with his heavenly Father. How can we, today, choose to cut into our busy schedules and demanding relationships? Is it possible to spend some moments each week with no agenda but to be with God? How can we see time alone as a place of transformation, where we are changed to relate to the world in a new and more godly way?

2) Simplicity

The second thing we notice about Jesus is how he rejects unnecessary baggage.

> "The devil led him up to a high place and showed him in an instant all the kingdoms of the world. And he said to him, 'I will give you all their authority and splendour; it has been given to me, and I can give it to anyone I want to.'" (Luke 4:5-6)

Jesus knows it is so easy to "gain the world" yet "lose your soul" (Luke 9:25), so he rebukes the devil. How many of the advertisements that surround us every day are about "gaining the world", or achieving more "authority and splendour"? How often are we tempted to buy yet more clothes, or upgrade to a better gadget, or invest in a bigger car?

Jesus was a homeless man (Luke 9:58). His only possessions seems to have been one set of clothes (John 19:23). When he sends out the 72 in Luke 10, he tells them: "Do not take a purse or bag or sandals" (10:4). It is not wrong for us to have homes, clothes and other possessions, but Jesus' example should cause us to question whether we need quite as many things as the adverts tell us we do.

Wilderness worship might ask us to consider whether we rely too much on things - even good things - instead of trusting in God. Maybe walking away from our warm homes and taking a prayer hike through the woods might help you see God afresh. Perhaps putting your smartphone away for a day might give you a new perspective on life and faith. Maybe turning off the music and the radio, sitting silently in God's presence, might be a form of simple, wilderness worship that restores your soul more than you realise.

3) Fasting

This leads us on to one of the most obvious things about Jesus' time in the wilderness - the fact that he fasted from food. The first temptation attacks this directly:

> "The devil said to him, 'If you are the Son of God, tell this stone to become bread.'" (Luke 5:3)

Notice that the devil doesn't say "You must be hungry", even though we know Jesus is feeling the effects of his forty day fast. He goes to the real heart of the matter - "If you are the Son of God..." Fasting is not about showing people how spiritual we are, or guilting God into answering our prayers. It comes down to the basis of our identity. Who are we, or perhaps more importantly whose are we? It reminds us that, more than food, our lives are sustained by the word of God, by Jesus the Word spoken to create us and in whom "all things hold together." (Col. 1:17). So Jesus responds using the words from Deuteronomy 8 that we read last week:

> "'Man shall not live on bread alone, but on every word that comes from the mouth of God.'" (Luke 5:4)

Now, literal fasting from food continued through the time of Jesus and into the early church (Matt. 9:15, Acts 13:2). It may be that during this Lent season you choose to give up some meal times, and to spend the time you would have been eating in prayer with God. If you have never tried it I would encourage you to start small and gradually build up.

But there are also other types of fast we can do. Isaiah 58:6 talks about a fast where people choose to put injustice right. 1 Corinthians 7:5 describes a fast where married couples refrain from physical intimacy for a time in order to focus on praying. These two things should show us that we can fast in other ways than from food.

Perhaps the question is: what would be the thing that you most rely on? Where are you in danger of getting your identity from, instead of God? Is it your social media account? The kinds of clothes you wear? Eating at particular restaurants? Or could you "fast" in a positive way like in Isaiah 58, by helping a homeless person on the street, befriending a lonely person at school, or standing up for a mistreated person at work?

RESPONSE IDEAS

Silence:

Engage with a longer silence after the talk, as suggested on page 18.

Commitment:

Give out small pieces of paper. Ask people to reflect for a moment on one practical thing they could do this week which would involve solitude, or simplicity, or fasting. Invite them to write that down on their paper and put it in their pocket, wallet or phone case. Pray that they would meet God as they engage in this act of wilderness worship.

SENDING IDEAS

Sending prayer:

> God, as we go from this place
> make us a people who are
> content in all circumstances:
> in crowds or alone,
> with much or with little,
> well-fed or hungry.
> May your presence, your provision
> and your bread of life be enough for us.
> In Christ's name we pray, Amen.

MUSIC IDEAS

Songs:

- *Simplicity* - Rend Collective
- *You Lead us Through The Wilderness* - Sam Hargreaves
- *Desert Song* - Brooke Ligertwood
- *When the Music Fades* - Matt Redman

Also, try simple songs which are well known to your congregation so that they require no books or projection - perhaps Taizé chants, charismatic choruses or repeated refrains from familiar hymns.

Hymns:

- *Jesus in the Desert* - David Mowbray
- *Forty Days and Forty Nights* - George H Smyttan
- *Jesus, Most Generous Lord* - Christopher Idle
- *Silent, Surrendered, Calm and Still* - Margaret Rizza
- *God is my Great Desire (Psalm 63)* - Timothy Dudley-Smith

Third Sunday

A SORROWFUL JOURNEY

"Crying is better than laughing.
It blotches the face but it scours the heart."
(Ecclesiastes 7:3, MSG)

GATHERING IDEA

Spoken prayer:

God, you rejoice with those who rejoice;
you mourn with those who mourn,
and you call us to do the same.
Help us to come to you today
with honesty and openness,
sharing our sorrows
and knowing your comfort.
Amen.

ALL-AGE IDEA

God who sees and hears:

Ask the congregation to share with a few people around them the things which make them sad. Then get feedback from the discussion. You can write the words down on a white board, or have someone type them up onto a projection screen. Explain briefly that God cares about the things which make us sad - his heart breaks when he sees broken situations in the world. Psalm 55:22 tells us to give our burdens to God because he cares for us.

Teach the following response:

[Leader:]
God, you know we feel sad about _____.
[All:]
You see our sorrows, [point to eye with finger, then run finger down face like a tear]

you hear our cries, [cup ear with one hand]

we lift our burdens to you. [two hands with palms up, lift up to God]

Then use the prayer, filling the blank with the things which were shared. If there are a lot, you can mention more than one in each gap.

PRAYER IDEA

Psalm 13 prayers of intercession:

This turns a lament psalm into corporate prayer for various groups who may be suffering in our world. Images are examples of the slides the congregation reads from.

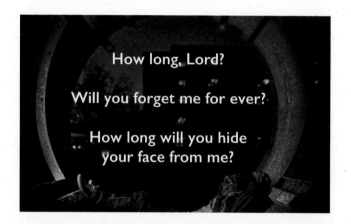

SLIDE 1 [Congregation:]
How long, Lord? Will you forget me for ever?
How long will you hide your face from me?

[Leader:]
We pray for those who feel forgotten and unseen, may they know that they are remembered and seen by you God.
Help us to partner with you to remember the forgotten.
Search our hearts to reveal those we hide our faces from, the outcast, the stranger or the homeless.
Change our hearts, that we may turn our faces towards these people and see them as your beloved children.

SLIDE 2 [Congregation:]
How long must I wrestle with my thoughts
   and day after day have sorrow in my heart?
How long will my enemy triumph over me?

[Leader:]
We pray for those we know who struggle with

 Downloadable PowerPoint   Downloadable Video   Downloadable Word Doc   Downloadable PDF Script mental illnesses, anxiety and depression. We pray that there will be resources released to help, enough staff employed and finances given towards mental health services nationally. Help us to be a friend and a listening ear to those who suffer. Fill us with compassion and wisdom.

Ultimately, we pray for those who wrestle with sorrow, that they may know your victory over those dark thoughts which currently seem to triumph.

SLIDE 3 [*Congregation:*]
Look on me and answer, Lord my God.
  Give light to my eyes, or I will sleep in death,
and my enemy will say, 'I have overcome him,'
  and my foes will rejoice when I fall.

[*Leader:*]
We pray for those who might be considered fallen by those around them: may they know your restoration and grace. Help us to not judge or exclude your beloved children, but instead lift them up in prayer, and embrace them with the grace we know in Christ.

Thank you, loving Father God, for hearing our prayer. We exclaim together:

SLIDE 4 [*Congregation:*]
But I trust in your unfailing love;
  my heart rejoices in your salvation.
I will sing the Lord's praise,
  for he has been good to me.

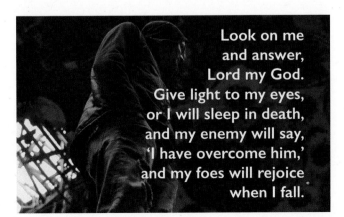

Look on me
and answer,
Lord my God.
Give light to my eyes,
or I will sleep in death,
and my enemy will say,
'I have overcome him,'
and my foes will rejoice
when I fall.

HEARING GOD'S WORD

Bible readings:

Exodus 3:1-10.

John 11:20-29, 32-36.

Sermon outline:

This week is perhaps the most difficult one on our journey through the wilderness. We began by talking about how the Holy Spirit of God calls us to the desert that we might be transformed. We have spoken about how wilderness worship looks different from mountaintop worship - it might involve things like solitude, silence and fasting. But this week we come to the stark truth that wilderness worship might also involve some sorrow.

1) The dangerous desert

Many of us will not have experienced the desert. If we live in cities, we may have a romanticised ideal of what living out in the wilderness might involve. But in Bible times there was no such misapprehension. Not only were deserts lacking in food and water, but these were not the only dangers, as Tom Wright also explains:

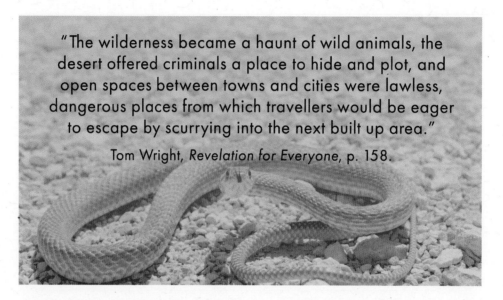

"The wilderness became a haunt of wild animals, the desert offered criminals a place to hide and plot, and open spaces between towns and cities were lawless, dangerous places from which travellers would be eager to escape by scurrying into the next built up area."

Tom Wright, *Revelation for Everyone*, p. 158.

For all these reasons, the wilderness was feared. For people in Bible times it represented the unknown, danger, failure and mortality.

Today we are not good at talking about, or reflecting on, these kinds of difficult issues. We all experience struggles, fears, doubts, disappointments, anger and hurt. All of us will at some point be faced with the mortality of ourselves and our loved ones. And yet so often we brush these thoughts under the carpet. British people will often do their best to keep a "stiff upper lip", to "keep calm and carry on". Even with God, we can come into church or to times of prayer, and try to pretend that everything is okay. Would God want to hear about our struggles? Can we be honest with him?

2) Learning to lament

Wilderness experiences in the Bible teach us that God does hear. He does care. In Exodus 3, Moses is hiding in the desert when he hears God say:

> "I have indeed seen the misery of my people in Egypt. I have heard them crying out because of their slave drivers, and I am concerned about their suffering." (Exodus 3:7)

Our God is not blind to our struggles or deaf to our cries. He does not consider it a lack of faith, an insult, or a sin if we choose to be honest with him. We can tell him about our doubts, how we feel about the state of the world, or even share when we feel disappointed with him. In fact, he wants his people to cry out to him in honesty and desperation. The Psalms are full of honest, raw complaint, sorrow and protest. Bible characters - from Hagar to

David, from Jesus to Paul, pray heartfelt prayers of distress. These prayers are called "lament".

Songwriter Michael Card describes the importance of the wilderness in teaching us to lament:

> "You and I were created to wake up in a garden. Instead we open our eyes each morning to a fallen wilderness, a world where our omnipresent God seems disturbingly absent... God transforms us and leads us by His grace into a pathway back to His presence. This path is found in the language of lament. When we lack the language to articulate this forsaken, fallen struggle, when we long for the words to cry out our confusion and bewilderment, the Bible provides such a language for us... Lament is learned only in the wilderness."
> Michael Card *"Worship in the Wilderness"* DTS Voice

3) Jesus meets us... and sends us

Lament will look different for each one of us. Some people will come and whisper a prayer. Others might shout at God. Some of us will sing a sad song, others might paint a canvas of our pain. Some of us will shake our fists, others will ask questions to try to understand.

We can see these different kinds of responses in our passages today. When Martha's brother dies she goes to Jesus with a theological question. Jesus meets her in that, he listens, he responds with a deep truth that she can place her hope in.

Mary is completely different. She has a question, but she mostly weeps. And so Jesus is moved deeply in his spirit and he weeps with her. Even though Jesus must know what he is about to do, he is profoundly sorrowful for Lazarus, and he is not afraid to show it.

> "When Jesus saw her weeping, and the Jews who had come along with her also weeping, he was deeply moved in spirit and troubled. 'Where have you laid him?' he asked. 'Come and see, Lord,' they replied. Jesus wept." (John 11:33-35)

The story of Moses demonstrates another of God's reactions to sorrowful circumstances. Moses isn't mourning a death - his issue is the mistreatment of his people under the Egyptians. But he is also consumed with self-doubt at the mistake he has already made in trying to sort this situation out. God comes to Moses to tell him that he cares, he heals, and that at he is calling Moses to do something about it.

So if you are like Martha, wilderness worship is a place for you to be honest with God. To tell him how you feel, to ask him questions, to call out "how long, O Lord?" All of these things are okay with him, and he will meet you in your honesty.

Wilderness worship is also a place to weep, to just let it all out like Mary did. That is okay with God too. Jesus stands and weeps with you.

And, thirdly, wilderness worship might be a place where God shows you his heart for a situation, as he did with Moses. God may move you for an injustice or a need or a person. It may be that he impresses his sorrow for something on your heart, and then he sends you to go and do something about it, in his power.

RESPONSE IDEAS

"We Have Come" reflective video:

This video will give space for people to engage with God honestly. Stills from the video can be seen below.

FROM YOU
NO SECRETS ARE HIDDEN.

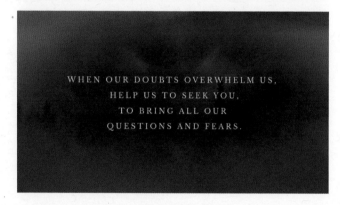

WHEN OUR DOUBTS OVERWHELM US,
HELP US TO SEEK YOU,
TO BRING ALL OUR
QUESTIONS AND FEARS.

SENDING IDEA

Sending prayer:

Thank you, gracious Father,
for the space to be honest with you today.
To you all hearts are open,
from you no secrets are hidden,
so may we continue to talk openly with you
as we go from this place.
Make us a people who listen to others,
sharing their sorrows,
and spreading your comfort.
In the power of your Spirit, amen.

Lament stations

To help people respond personally and privately, you could set up a number of stations in the church. These could include:

1) Provide a number of trays of sand. Invite people to write their honest prayer of lament in the sand, knowing that God sees and hears when we come to him with what is on our hearts.

2) Re-write a psalm of lament. You could provide copies of psalms such as 22 and 88, and invite people to re-write these in their own words, reflecting their own situations.

3) Lament for the persecuted church. In Revelation 6:9-10 the martyrs cry out to God "How long", asking for justice. You could print stories of the persecuted Christians around the world today, and invite people to write or speak out prayers for justice today.

4) Prayer ministry. This week's theme might bring up some deep issues, so it could be helpful to have a trained prayer ministry team available to chat and pray with people.

MUSIC IDEAS

Songs:

- *Hear this Broken Cry* - Sunil Chandy
- *Lord You Hear the Cry (Lord Have Mercy)* - Geraldine Latty
- *You Are a Refuge (Arms)* - Ben Atkins
- *Out of the Depths* - Rachel Wilhelm
- *Why So Downcast, O My Soul* - Sam Hargreaves
- *We Have Come to our Father* - Sam Hargreaves
- *When God's Perfect Plans* - Andy Clarke

Hymns:

- *Abide With Me* - Henry Francis Lyte
- *All the Brown and Bare Horizons* - Christopher Idle

Fourth Sunday

A SACRIFICIAL JOURNEY

"Do good and share with others,
for with such sacrifices God is pleased"
(Hebrews 13:16)

GATHERING IDEAS

Spoken prayer:

Jesus, you made the way
for us to come and worship the Father.
As we see your sacrifice,
lead us in the way of the wilderness,
the way of the cross,
the way that leads to eternal life.
Amen.

"Let us Kneel" video:

Watch this video and reflect on the sacrifice Jesus has made on the cross.

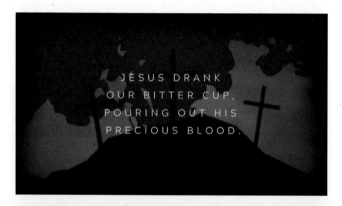

JESUS DRANK OUR BITTER CUP, POURING OUT HIS PRECIOUS BLOOD.

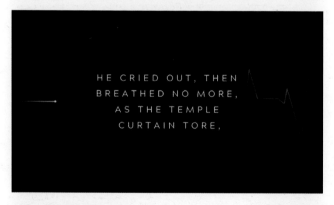

HE CRIED OUT, THEN BREATHED NO MORE, AS THE TEMPLE CURTAIN TORE,

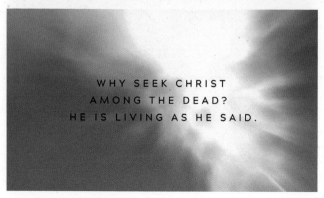

WHY SEEK CHRIST AMONG THE DEAD? HE IS LIVING AS HE SAID.

HEARING GOD'S WORD

Isaiah 52-53 with interjections:

Written by Bob Hartman, used with permission.

This is designed so that one person reads the Bible text, whilst another makes interjections to help people reflect on the text. In an all-age context, the Reader 2 parts could be said by someone playing a character.

[*Reader 1*] Read Isaiah 52:13-15

[*Reader 2*] "Shocked. Are you ready to be shocked? God's servant. Marred. Disfigured. Hardly human, by the look of him. Yet chosen to do God's will. Chosen to be exalted. Shocked. Are you ready to be shocked?"

[*Reader 1*] Read Isaiah 53:1-3

[*Reader 2*] "Suffering. Can you see him suffering? Despised. Rejected. Ugly. Misshapen. Devoid of anything that might remotely be considered attractive. Can you bear to look at him? Can you stomach what happened to him? Does it make any sense that God should be at work in him? Suffering. Can you see him suffering?"

[*Reader 1*] Read Isaiah 53:4-6

[*Reader 2*] "Blame. Will you take the blame? That the ugliness and the pain, the bruises and the beatings, were your fault and mine? And were meant, most of all, to take the blame away. Blame? Yes, he took the blame."

[*Reader 1*] Read Isaiah 53:7

[*Reader 2*] "Silence. Can you bear the silence? The innocent lamb, the shears, and the abattoir. No bleating. No protest. Silence. Can you bear the silence?"

[*Reader 1*] Read Isaiah 53:8-9

[*Reader 2*] "Injustice. Do you feel the injustice? An innocent man condemned to death. A man of peace crushed by violence. An honest man entombed with liars. Injustice. Do you feel the injustice?

[*Reader 1*] Read Isaiah 53:10-12

[*Reader 2*] "Hope. Can you find the hope? Can you see how God could be in this? And that, through the pain of his servant, he could bring hope to you and to me. And to his servant, too? That there might be light at the end of all this darkness. Victory beyond imagining from unimaginable suffering? Hope. Can you find the hope?"

Bible readings:

Isaiah 53:1-12. A paraphrased version of this reading is available as a reflective PowerPoint that you can download. See example images below.

Matthew 14:13-14.

He grew up like a tender shoot
through the desert sand.

Like lost sheep, we have all forsaken
the path and wandered off,
and the shepherd has paid the price
for all our waywardness.

After walking that dark road,
He will be vindicated when he
steps into the light once again,
and sees the fruit of his suffering.

He was cut off from the land of the living and buried amongst the wicked and the rich, though he had done no wrong.

Sermon Outline:

"Sacrifice" is not a popular term to speak about. Our lives are hard enough, busy enough, without the extra struggle of choosing to go without something we feel we need. Perhaps some here have made a sacrifice over Lent to not enjoy something which they usually have in their lives; whether that be chocolate, beer or social media. Has that been difficult?

Does God demand that we give things up for him, or choose difficult, "sacrificial" paths in order to please him?

In order to understand what sacrifice means, we turn to chapter 53 of Isaiah, and then turn to Hebrews for the New Testament outworking for us today. Isaiah foretold, hundreds of years before the birth of Jesus, a type of Messiah who was not the strong and powerful leader which Jesus' contemporaries were expecting. Sometimes the text was thought to represent the nation of Israel and its suffering, but later the New Testament writers understood it to be about Jesus.

1) Jesus, the man of sorrows

We already saw last week how Jesus meets us in our different states of distress. Yet, we read in this chapter that Jesus does more than just provide a shoulder for us to cry on. The journey of Jesus himself was one of sorrow as he travelled through the wilderness of this world, a journey which ultimately took him to the very epicentre of wilderness: the cross.

Isaiah prophesied about Jesus that he was:

> "like a root in dry ground....
> He was despised and rejected—
> a man of sorrows, acquainted with deepest grief." (Isaiah 53:2-3)

We know that this man of sorrows wept at Lazarus' tomb, wept over the fate of Jerusalem (Luke 19:41), and mourned the loss of his cousin, John the Baptist. In Matthew 14 we hear the horrible story of John being beheaded. When Jesus hears this news about his cousin he takes himself away to a desert place (verse 13). He chooses to go to the desert to mourn before his heavenly Father. Our God knows intimately the human experience of grief and pain. This is part of who Jesus is.

2) Jesus, the sacrificial lamb

Isaiah foretold that the Messiah would not only know our sorrow, but that he would carry the full weight of our suffering, sin and shame.

> "Surely he took up our pain and bore our suffering...
> the punishment that brought us peace was on him,
> and by his wounds we are healed." (Isaiah 53:4)

Isaiah's words contain many echoes of the Day of Atonement in Leviticus 16. This passage from Israel's 40 years in the wilderness tells of how God dealt with their sin, one day each year, through the death of a sacrificial lamb and the sacrifice of a "scapegoat". The priest would place his hands on the head of the goat to transfer the guilt of the people onto it. It was then sent away to symbolically carry the weight of all Israel's sin out into the wilderness: "The goat will carry on itself all their sins to a solitary place" (verse 22). It was to be "cut off from the land of the living", suffering for these sins so the people didn't have to. Echoing this story, Isaiah writes:

> "He was led like a lamb to the slaughter,
> and as a sheep before its shearers is silent,

so he did not open his mouth.
By oppression and judgment he was taken away.
Yet who of his generation protested?
For he was cut off from the land of the living;
for the transgression of my people he was punished." (Isaiah 53:7-8)

Whatever wilderness you struggle with, Jesus has born the pain of that, on his shoulders on the cross. He has become your scapegoat, carrying your sin, your struggles, your sorrows. He went out into the wilderness of judgement all alone, so that ultimately we may all be healed, restored and made whole.

3) The sacrifices we are called to make

The book of Hebrews is a good place to go to in the New Testament to help us understand how Jesus continues and concludes the story of the Old Testament. In chapter 10, the writer describes how Jesus completely fulfils all that the Day of Atonement was pointing towards; that Jesus is the one, final sacrifice for all sin, and that:

"... by one sacrifice he has made perfect for ever those who are being made holy." (Hebrews 10:14)

We cannot make ourselves right with God - only Jesus has done that. Therefore, any sacrifices we bring today are not given in order to earn God's favour. And yet the writer to the Hebrews does say that there are sacrifices we are called to make. We are called to make sacrifices of praise, and sacrifices of doing good and sharing with other people.

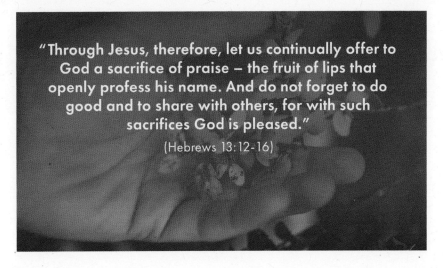

"Through Jesus, therefore, let us continually offer to God a sacrifice of praise – the fruit of lips that openly profess his name. And do not forget to do good and to share with others, for with such sacrifices God is pleased."

(Hebrews 13:12-16)

The sacrifice we bring is the sacrifice of response. Seeing how Jesus has dealt with our sorrow and shame, we are inspired and empowered to bring our praise and our service. We can worship God with our lips in songs and prayers, and we can worship God with generosity and compassion towards other people.

MUSIC IDEAS

Songs:

- *Come See the Son* - Joel Payne
- *Let us Kneel at Calvary* - Sam Hargreaves
- *Lamb of God* - Judy Gresham
- *I Will Offer up my Life* - Matt Redman
- *The Servant King* - Graham Kendrick
- *Send us Out* - Matt Osgood

Hymns:

- *When I Survey* - Isaac Watts
- *Here is Love* - William Rees

RESPONSE IDEAS

Communion:

This week would be an ideal one to share Holy Communion together. You will need to honour your church's traditions and structures, but can you also focus on the sacrifice of Jesus as we see it in Isaiah 53? And can you make connections between Jesus' sacrifice and our commitment to pour out our own lives for other people?

Acts of kindness:

Invite people to think about an act of kindness they could do this week, a small sacrifice which would make a difference to someone else. What is one way we could share the blessings of God's love with the people around us:

- Buy a gift for someone at work and leave it on their desk.
- Write an encouraging card or letter to someone.
- Share some money with someone who is in need.
- Buy food for a homeless person.
- Invite someone who might be lonely over for dinner.

Ask people to share their idea with one person around them, and to pray for each other that we might be able to make this small sacrifice for God's glory and to bless another person.

SENDING IDEA

Sending prayer:

Written by Mark Earey, used with permission.

[*Leader:*] See my Servant, says the God of hope,
[*All:*] **wounded, scarred and broken.**

[*Leader:*] Many shall see and be astonished:
nations, startled and shocked,
their leaders staring and speechless.
He was wounded to bring wholeness.

[*Leader:*] Come my servant, says the God of hope,
[*All:*] **wounded, scarred and broken.**

[*Leader:*] Go into a world which is battered and bruised,
its peoples hungry and without hope.
Walk with my people, and bring wholeness.

God of hope, you sent Jesus,
wounded, scarred and broken,
to walk with us.
[*All:*] **Send us now,
your wounded, scarred and broken church,
to bring wholeness and hope. Amen.**

Fifth Sunday

A TRUTH-SPEAKING JOURNEY

"But the word of our God stands forever...
Shout it louder, O Jerusalem"
(Isaiah 40:8-9)

GATHERING IDEA

Spoken prayer:

God, we may come to you dry,
discouraged, feeling frail or powerless.
But we come believing that you have
the words of eternal life.
Speak to our dry bones,
may your Word and your Spirit give us life,
and empower us to speak truth
into this world you love.
Amen.

ALL-AGE IDEA
"A Tempting Time" reading:

Written by Dave Hopwood, used with permission.

An interactive story for all ages. Teach the responses before
reading the story and then allow pauses for everyone to
join in. This can also be led by a group at the front who
lead all the responses.

First - Hold up one finger and shout "One".

Second - Hold up two fingers and shout "Two".

Third - Hold up three fingers and shout "Three".

Fourth - Hold up four fingers and shout "Four".

Rocks - Make a fist as if it's a rock and beat it on
other palm.

Wild Animals - Make wild animal sounds.

Words - Hold two hands like an open book and
blow gently on them.

Before Jesus could begin his work he went through a
series of challenges.
First: He went out into the wilderness where he had
to survive all on his own, with no one else around.
Second: He had no food and he was out there for
forty days, so he felt very weak and hungry by the
end of that time.
Third: There were **wild animals** out there, and he
had to trust God to keep him safe.
Fourth: He had to face three difficult tests.

The **first** was this: he was tempted by the devil to
turn the **rocks** around him into lovely soft fresh
bread. As he was very hungry this was a very
difficult test. He could easily have done it with all
the power that he had, he could have turned the
rocks into all kinds of delicious food, but he didn't.
Instead he remembered and spoke these **words**:
"It takes more than bread to stay alive - we need to
have God's life-giving **words**."

The **second** test was this: he found himself on top of
the temple in the city and was tempted by the devil
to make a spectacular jump. God would have to
send some angels to catch him, so that he wouldn't
even stub his toe on the **rocks** below. People in the
city would see it and it would prove that he was the
Son of God. But Jesus remembered and spoke these
words: "Whatever you do: don't test God, trust
him."

The **third** test happened like this: he walked up onto
the **rocks** overlooking miles and miles of beautiful
cities. The devil said to him, "You can have all this.
All of it, you can be in charge of it all. All you have
to do is worship me instead of God."

The idea of all the cities being under his control was
very tempting, but instead Jesus remembered and
spoke these **words**: "Worship God, he is the Lord
of heaven and earth and he is the only one we must
ever worship."

Jesus knew that he already had all the power in the
world: he didn't have to prove it. After this, God
sent his angels to look after Jesus and keep him safe
from the **wild animals**.

INTERCESSION IDEA

Praying for your town:

Buy or draw a large map of your town and put it at the
front of the church. Ask the congregation to express in just
a few words some of the needs, struggles and sins in your
town - poverty, loneliness, broken families, and so on.
Write these on the map. Then invite people to find Bible

verses which speak truth, life and love over those words you have written down. Hand out post-it notes, and invite people to write those verses on the notes and then stick them over the map, so that God's truth is covering over the sins and struggles. You could then pray some of those truths out loud.

Additionally you could use a sung refrain to sing out prayers over your town - "Come Lord Jesus" from the song *"Great is the Darkness"*, or *"Build Your Kingdom Here"* from the Rend Collective song, or a setting of *Kyrie Eleison* or "Lord Have Mercy".

HEARING GOD'S WORD

"Those Dry Bones Get Everywhere" poem:

Written by Dave Hopwood, used with permission.

This poem can be read reflectively, alongside the visuals of the PowerPoint (example to the right), to help people apply the message to their everyday situations.

Those dry bones get everywhere.
In the workplaces and job centres, in the homes and high streets, in the schools and colleges.

Those dry bones get everywhere.
In the shops and sports arenas, in the places of entertainment and the centres of leisure.

Those dry bones get everywhere.
Sprinkling their lifeless dust,
sapping energy and draining hope,
confusing minds and sowing discontent

Those dry bones get everywhere -
but so does the breath of God,
and so does the hopeful life of the Spirit.

Gentle and powerful,
rushing and meandering,
transforming radically, and little by little,
resurrecting, encouraging, stirring, comforting.

Those dry bones get everywhere -
but so does the breath of God.

"Hearing the Word" prayer:

For this prayer, encourage the congregation to hold a Bible or a device with the Bible in it. If they don't have one they can just make the gestures with their hands.

[*Hold the Bible in your open palms.*]
[*Leader:*] Generous God, the Bible is your gift to us:
[*All:*] **We choose to receive your story with thanks**.

[*Hold the Bible in front of your mouth.*]
[*Leader:*] Providing God, your word is daily bread for us:
[*All:*] **Help us to hunger for your words of life.**

[*Hold the Bible over your heart.*]
[*Leader:*] Challenging God, your word is living and active:
[*All:*] **Open us up to receive your truth in our hearts.**

[*Hold the Bible behind one ear.*]
[*Leader:*] Comforting God, your word sings out your everlasting love:
[*All:*] **Tune our ears to the frequency of your song**

[*Hold the Bible out in front of you, pointing the way.*]
[*Leader:*] Guiding God, your word is a light to our path:
[*All:*] **May we reflect on your ways, and then walk in them. Amen.**

Bible readings:

Ezekiel 37:1-14.

Matthew 4:4-11.

Sermon outline:

We have explored in our series the wilderness worship that God can lead us into - things like silence, fasting and solitude. We have also thought about sorrow in the desert, the sacrifice Jesus has made to bear our suffering and the sacrifices we're called to make as a response.

Lots of these ideas picture wilderness as a spiritual state in our hearts. In addition to these, you may also feel that the world around you is something of a wilderness. We do live in an increasingly secular society. Christian voices can seem to be more marginalised than ever. Christian values may not be shared by your family, or your work colleagues, or by the people who run the newspapers, TV stations and websites you look at. It can feel like we're bombarded with temptations to live in ways that are the opposite of God's best for us, and we may struggle to resist.

Do you ever feel like a lone voice in the wilderness? How can we be inspired by Isaiah, and by John the Baptist all those years later, to be:

> "a voice of one calling: in the wilderness prepare the way for the Lord;
> make straight in the desert a highway for our God." (Isaiah 40:3)?

1) Wilderness and exile

The Israelites' 40 years in the wilderness was a defining period for God's people, and a lasting demonstration of God's character towards them. His faithfulness to them during that time was a theme they would return to again and again. In times of crisis they would bring to mind their experience in the desert and use it as a lens for seeing how God might act in their present trouble.

This was certainly the case when Israel was taken into exile by Babylon in 597 BC. There could have been no greater crisis than to be ripped out of the "promised land" and ten years later to have the city and its temple destroyed. God's people were distraught. And yet prophets like Jeremiah, Isaiah and Ezekiel tried to remind the people that, even in the desert of exile, they could still rely on the God who had brought them through the wilderness.

In Ezekiel's vision, the people are not simply hungry and thirsty in the desert of exile. They are dead, their bodies have rotted away, and only their bones are left on the dry, dusty desert floor. Yes, a rather disgusting image. But this is the extent of Israel's despair. Look at verse 11:

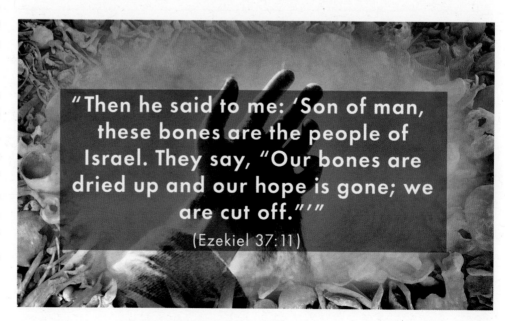

"Then he said to me: 'Son of man, these bones are the people of Israel. They say, "Our bones are dried up and our hope is gone; we are cut off."'"
(Ezekiel 37:11)

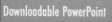 

Does that image of exile relate to the despair you sometimes feel about the world around you? About our society, and a church that seems increasingly marginalised and ignored? If it resonates with you at all, then you can take heart from what happens through Ezekiel.

2) The power of the prophetic Word

God calls Ezekiel to speak to the dead bones. He speaks God's creative, restorative word, and the dead bones come together, muscles and flesh grow back over them. He speaks again and God's life giving Spirit comes and brings life to the dead.

> "So I prophesied as he commanded me, and breath entered them; they came to life and stood up on their feet—a vast army." (Ezekiel 37:10)

The dejected, dead people of Israel are resurrected. They become an army, a people who will re-occupy their promised land. God's Word and his Spirit do what no other power, politician, product or programme could do - bring new and true life.

If we are looking to bring transformation to the world around us - to our churches, to our homes, to our workplaces, our pubs, our schools - we need to know God's word and we need to speak it in the power of his Holy Spirit. This means we need to regularly read the Bible - soaking ourselves in it and trying to understand it better. It means speaking God's truth in love. It means praying with prophetic faith - speaking out God's word with the trust that it will be effective. It means reminding ourselves of God's promises whenever we get dejected. And, as Jesus show us, it means using God's word to respond to temptation.

3) Speaking truth to temptation

When Jesus is led into the desert, it seems that he also understands his 40 days in the light of Israel's 40 years of wilderness wandering. When we looked at Deuteronomy 8 we saw that the reason God gives for Israel's wilderness wanderings was:

> "to teach you that man does not live on bread alone but on every word that comes from the mouth of the Lord." (Deuteronomy 8:3)

Each time Jesus is tempted by the devil he responds by quoting the word of God - in fact he even uses scriptures from Deuteronomy which refer to Israel's wilderness testing (8:3, 6:13, 16). So Jesus stands where Israel fell. And in doing so he shows us Christians - the New Israel - how we can also stand in the face of temptation.

We do not have a specific forty years or forty days of temptation. For us, each day holds an opportunity to obey or disobey God's best for our lives. What kinds of sins are you tempted to commit in your everyday life? What truths from God's word can you speak to resist those temptations?

As we do this, we are obeying that call of Isaiah to be voices calling in the wilderness. We can be those who proclaim to the world:

> "The grass withers and the flowers fade,
> but the word of our God stands forever."...
> Shout it louder, O Jerusalem.
> Shout, and do not be afraid.
> Tell the towns of Judah,
> "Your God is coming!" (Isaiah 40:8-9 NLT)

RESPONSE IDEAS

Take it to heart:

Print out the downloadable sheets with Bible verses on, cut them out and put them into bowls. During the service, pass the bowls around and suggest that as a response people choose one verse from the bowl. They can then commit to trying to learn these words off by heart, and speaking them out in their lives when they feel tempted, disappointed or fearful.

"Word of God" responsive prayer:

Written by Sharon Tedford, used with permission.

This prayer helps us confess times we have not engaged with God's word as we could, and commits us to living by God's word in the future.

[*Leader:*] Father, when I come to you hungry,
Perhaps it's because I haven't fed properly from your word.
[*All:*] **Word of God, feed me.**

[*Leader:*] There are times when I lose my way;
I feel like I'm going round in circles, unsure of my next step.
[*All:*] **Word of God, lead me.**

[*Leader:*] When I'm stuck in repetitive habits,
I know that you have more for me outside of this mediocrity.
[*All:*] **Word of God, shake me.**

[*Leader:*] Parts of my heart are cold towards the world you love.
Fill me with your compassion.
[*All:*] **Word of God, break me**

[*Leader:*] "The word of God is living and active, sharper than any double edged sword."

[*All:*] **Feed me with your wisdom,**
lead me with your love,
shake me with your reality,
break me with your perspective
and rebuild me with your Holy Spirit's power.
Amen.

SENDING IDEA

Sending prayer:

Holy Spirit, breathe through us,
so that we might speak out
words of light and life
where we see only shadows and death.
Send us into this world of exile
with the promise of a world renewed
and the power of our risen saviour,
in whose name we pray, amen.

MUSIC IDEAS

Songs:

- *Your Word O Lord* - Chris Pearse
- *We Come to Hear Your Word* - Chris Juby
- *Ashes* - Mia Fildes, Jason Ingram
- *Come Alive (Dry Bones)* - Lauren Daigle, Michael Farren
- *Dry Bones* - Nikki Fletcher, Tim Hughes, Tom Smith
- *Speak O Lord* - Keith Getty, Stuart Townend

Hymns:

- *Tell Out My Soul* - Timothy Dudley Smith
- *Word of God, Renew Your People* - Bernadette Farrell

Palm Sunday

A SURPRISING JOURNEY

"The desert and the parched land
will be glad; the wilderness will
rejoice and blossom"
(Isaiah 35:1)

GATHERING IDEA

Spoken prayer:

> We welcome you, King Jesus,
> humble king, king of our lives,
> with shouts of "hosanna"
> for you are the God who saves.
> We fix our eyes on you, King Jesus,
> the pioneer and perfecter of faith,
> our hope of a wilderness restored.
> Amen.

ALL-AGE IDEAS

Palm Sunday interactive reading:

Written by Bob Hartman, used with permission.

Break your group into the following small groups and teach them the following actions/words. When the time comes for them to speak, point to them and lead them in their actions/words. You might need to put the longer lines up on a screen.

Young donkey - put hands at side of head as ears, wiggle ears and say "hee-haw".

Donkey owner - hands on hips, or scratching head, "Why are you untying my donkey?"

Two disciples - shrug shoulders and say, "The Lord needs it."

People - pretend to spread cloaks with whooshing sound.

All disciples - shout "Blessed is the King who comes in God's name. Hosanna in the highest."

Pharisees - shaking finger "Tell your disciples to be quiet!"

Stones - "You can't always get what you want, but if you try sometimes, you might just find you get what you need."

After Jesus had said these things, he went up to Jerusalem. When he got close to Bethpage and Bethany, at a place called The Mount of Olives, he called two of his disciples and gave them the following orders:

"Go into the village, up ahead. When you get there, you will find a young donkey (**young donkey group** - put hands at side of head as ears, wiggle ears and say "hee-haw") that has never been ridden. It will be tied up. So you need to untie it and bring it to me.

If the owner asks you (**donkey owner group** - hands on hips, or scratching head, "Why are you untying my donkey?"), simply tell him (**two disciples group** - shrug shoulders and say, "The Lord needs it.")".

The disciples did as Jesus told them. They went into the village. They found the young donkey (**young donkey group** - put hands at side of head as ears, wiggle ears and say "hee-haw"). And they started to untie it. But, as they did so, the owner came up to them and asked, (**donkey owner group** - hands on hips, or scratching head, "Why are you untying my donkey?").

And just as Jesus had told them to do, they replied, (**two disciples group** - shrug shoulders and say, "The Lord needs it.").

Then the two disciples brought the young donkey (**young donkey group** - put hands at side of head as ears, wiggle ears and say "hee-haw") to Jesus. They put their cloaks on it, set Jesus on its back, and off he rode.

As Jesus rode along, people spread their cloaks on the road, in front of him. (**People** - pretend to spread cloaks with whooshing sound.)

They reached the path that led down from the Mount of Olives into Jerusalem. And the whole multitude of disciples began to shout praises to Jesus for all the powerful things they had seen him do. (**All disciples** - shout "Blessed is the King who comes in God's name. Hosanna in the highest.")

When the Pharisees heard this, they were not very happy. Some of them called to Jesus, saying (**Pharisees** - shaking finger "Tell your disciples to be quiet!").

To which Jesus simply replied, "If you managed somehow to quiet this lot, the stones themselves would shout out." (**Stones** - "You can't always get what you want, but if you try sometimes, you might just find you get what you need.")

Which was actually truer than any of them knew. What Jesus actually meant, of course, was that the stones would shout out his praises, too. So let's all do it together. **Donkeys, Pharisees, everyone**:

"Blessed is the King who comes in God's name! Hosanna in the highest!"

"Heroes of Faith" gallery:

Hebrews 11 lists many heroes and heroines of the Old Testament. Give out pieces of A4 paper and pens (these could have a "frame" printed around the outside). Invite everyone to draw a picture of one of their "Heroes of Faith", with the name of their hero as a caption. It could be someone from the Bible, someone from history or someone they know today.

To develop this one step further, invite them to write down one "victory" and one "struggle" their hero experienced. This will be echoed in Hebrews 11:32-40, where the Old Testament heroes experienced both victories and great hardships. Then stick all the pictures to a wall and invite everyone to look at the different pictures, and talk about the different struggles these heroes faced.

HEARING GOD'S WORD
Isaiah 35 visual reflection: ⬇

This PowerPoint can be used reflectively to express the joy of Isaiah 35, the promise of the desert wasteland being turned into a glorious place of life. See examples to right.

The desert and the parched land will be glad; the wilderness will rejoice and blossom.

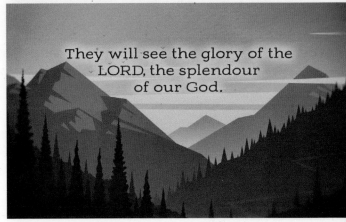

They will see the glory of the LORD, the splendour of our God.

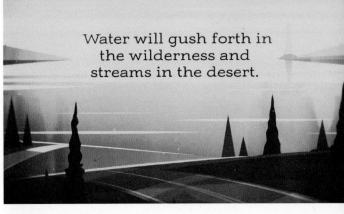

Water will gush forth in the wilderness and streams in the desert.

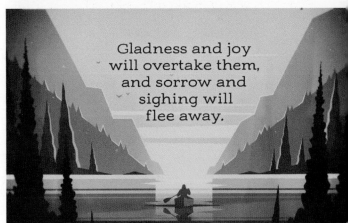

Gladness and joy will overtake them, and sorrow and sighing will flee away.

Bible readings:

Hebrews 11:32-40.

Matthew 21:1-11.

Sermon outline:

We are reaching the end of our journey through the wilderness, and heading into what is called Holy Week. We've been preparing ourselves to journey with Jesus into his most difficult and barren period yet - his betrayal, trial, crucifixion and death. We, of course, know the end of the story - that the horror of Good Friday and the numb waiting of Easter Saturday will explode with joy into the victorious resurrection of Sunday morning. But for those who lived through that first Easter weekend, the struggle of this week was all too real. They had no way to be sure it would all turn out okay.

Our own wilderness experiences can be very much like that. Looking back, we can see how God has used dry, barren and difficult times to shape us. But when we are in the middle of them it is almost impossible to get that kind of perspective. And when good things come along they can take us by complete surprise, as God works in mysterious and unpredictable ways.

1) Surprising hope in the Old Testament

When we read the account in Hebrews 11 of the "heroes of the Old Testament" we get this kind of picture. The writer describes giants of faith, who nevertheless lived through some literal and metaphorical wilderness experiences. It says:

> "Some faced jeers and flogging, and even chains and imprisonment. They were put to death by stoning; they were sawn in two; they were killed by the sword. They went about in sheepskins and goatskins, destitute, persecuted and ill-treated – the world was not worthy of them. They wandered in deserts and mountains, living in caves and in holes in the ground." (Hebrews 11:36-38)

These were not super-spiritual people who floated through life on a cloud. They struggled in the deserts of sorrow, rejection and physical violence. In the midst of this, the writer records some amazing answers to prayer. We are told that they were people who:

> "through faith conquered kingdoms, administered justice, and gained what was promised; who shut the mouths of lions, quenched the fury of the flames, and escaped the edge of the sword; whose weakness was turned to strength; and who became powerful in battle and routed foreign armies. Women received back their dead, raised to life again." (Hebrews 11:33-35)

They did see amazing answers to their prayers and their acts of faith. But when the writer comes to the end of the account, they admit that:

> "These were all commended for their faith, yet none of them received what had been promised, since God had planned something better for us so that only together with us would they be made perfect." (Hebrews 11:39-40)

2) Fulfilment in Jesus

The fulfilment that these fathers and mothers in the faith were looking for was only going to come in Jesus. The hopes of the people of God were pinned on this surprising Messiah. He comes, not as a military superpower but

as a helpless baby. He lives, not as a rich politician but as a homeless wanderer. He preaches, not vengeance to Israel's oppressors but grace and love for enemies. And his triumphant entry into Jerusalem is not on a chariot of war, but fulfils the prophesy of Zechariah from hundreds of years before:

> "Rejoice greatly, Daughter Zion!
> Shout, Daughter Jerusalem!
> See, your king comes to you,
> righteous and victorious,
> lowly and riding on a donkey,
> on a colt, the foal of a donkey." (Zechariah 9:9)

The surprising answer to all of Israel's hopes is a humble man on a donkey. A humble man, who would further humble himself to die on a cross. The crowd who welcomed him with palm branches and shouts of "Hosanna" would quickly turn on him. The cross that appeared to be his final defeat would turn out to be his final victory over death, sin and the devil. His resurrection would become the first fruits of the resurrection of all things. It is the guarantee of the promise through Isaiah:

> "The desert and the parched land
> will be glad;
> the wilderness will rejoice and blossom...
> Water will gush forth in the wilderness
> and streams in the desert.
> The burning sand will become a pool,
> the thirsty ground bubbling springs...
> Gladness and joy will overtake them,
> and sorrow and sighing will flee away."
> (Isaiah 35:1, 6-7, 10)

The burning sand will become a pool, the thirsty ground bubbling springs.

3) Living in the in-between

And where do we live now? We live in the in-between. Jesus is risen. Death is defeated. We have the salvation of Christ and the power of the Holy Spirit. And yet, God hasn't quite finished with this "wilderness world". He holds back Christ's final coming, and so we continue to experience both desert struggles and resurrection surprises. The promised land is before us, so the writer to the Hebrews encourages us to take heart from the Old Testament heroes and from Jesus, to finish this journey together:

> "Therefore, since we are surrounded by such a great cloud of witnesses, let us throw off everything that hinders and the sin that so easily entangles. And let us run with perseverance the race marked out for us, fixing our eyes on Jesus, the pioneer and perfecter of faith. For the joy that was set before him he endured the cross, scorning its shame, and sat down at the right hand of the throne of God. Consider him who endured such opposition from sinners, so that you will not grow weary and lose heart." (Hebrews 12:1-3)

Journeying with Jesus means drawing strength from him during the hard times. We can know that he has walked this wilderness road before us, and that he is walking with us now. He is using even our struggles to transform us, and to prepare us for the day when all sorrow and sighing will flee away.

RESPONSE IDEAS

Group discussion:

Invite people to get into groups and discuss the following questions:

- Do you relate to the heroes of faith in Hebrews - experiencing both victories and struggles? Which are more common right now?

- Have you experienced any surprising answers to prayer?

- Has anything been new or helpful to you during this Lent season of journeying through the wilderness?

- What can the group pray for you as you come to the end of this term, and journey through this Easter season?

Allow space for people to pray for one another in their groups.

"Heroes of Faith" gallery:

If you began the gallery suggested on page 43, you could continue this with self-portraits. Invite people to depict how they feel before God right now. They can also write one struggle and one victory on the paper, and then add their image to the gallery.

Then ask everyone to look at the gallery and to pray for the people that they see there.

SENDING IDEA

Sending prayer:

Jesus, we have walked with you this far.
May we not abandon you in this Holy Week,
but stay by your side through your sorrow,
that we might also join you for your resurrection morning.
Surprise us on this journey,
as we fix our eyes on you,
author and perfecter of our faith. Amen.

MUSIC IDEAS

Songs:

- *Praise is Rising* - Brenton Brown, Paul Baloche
- *Hosanna* - Brooke Fraser
- *Come and Worship Christ the King* - Chris Juby
- *Christ Was Raised* - Sam Hargreaves

Hymns:

- *All Glory Praise and Honour* - Theodulf of Orleans
- *There's a Man Riding in on a Donkey* - Paul Wigmore
- *Ride On, Ride On in Majesty* - H H Milman
- *Let the Desert Sing and the Wasteland Flower* - Michael Perry